LOVE, LIFE, AND RELATIONSHIPS

Poems From A Young Girl's Heart

Grace LaJoy Henderson

Inspirations by Grace LaJoy
www.gracelajoy.com
poetry@gracelajoy.com

Love, Life, and Relationships *Grace LaJoy Henderson*

Cover by Grace LaJoy Henderson

LOVE, LIFE, AND RELATIONSHIPS
Copyright © 2013. Grace LaJoy Henderson
Published by Inspirations by Grace LaJoy
www.gracelajoy.com

ISBN 978-0-9829404-8-8

All rights reserved. No portion of this book may be copied, reproduced or transmitted in any form without prior written permission from the publisher.

Printed in the United States of America

DEDICATION

I dedicate this book to my two children Aric and Arica.

ACKNOWLEDGMENTS

I acknowledge God for the gift of creative writing that He gave me; and for enabling me to express my inner-most feelings through poetry.

I acknowledge my siblings, Chrystal, Darlene, James, Gregory, and Tyrone.

I acknowledge my sister-in-laws, Paula and Sharon.

I acknowledge my father James, who died in 1990; and my mother Gloria Dawn, whom I do not know. Although I grew up without my mother, I acknowledge her because she gave me life.

A special acknowledgment to my sister, Chrystal, who encouraged me by listening to my poems and songs when I was young. She said to me, "You have a gift! Everybody can't write poems like that."

FOREWORD

When I read the poems in **Love, Life and Relationships**, they made me feel good! They are very, very personal and I could identify with them. They touched my love life. The poems are very deep and sincere; I believe they will touch the emotions of every reader.

I also believe high school and college students will be able to relate to these poems. People don't readily talk freely about these types of feelings and emotions. The poems in this book opens the door for the reader to get in touch with hidden emotions; and to openly discuss issues of the heart that are not readily talked about at home and school.

Dr. Sugar Lee Lewis, Author
A New Kind of Hustle:
Finding Success in the Midst of Obstacles
Retired Public School Administrator

Love, Life, and Relationships *Grace LaJoy Henderson*

TABLE OF CONTENTS

WATCHING YOU..........1	A KISS FROM YOU..……...14
YOUR HEART……….....2	A KISS FROM ME………...14
VIRGINITY ……………. .2	A CHILD AND YOU…..…..15
LOVE CONTRACT……....3	KIM AND MICHAEL….…...15
MY EVERYTHING……….4	IF TOMORROW COMES TOO LATE………………...16
JUST BECAUSE………….5	
OUR LOVE…………….6	IF TOMORROW NEVER COMES …………..17
SOONER OR LATER….…..7	I AM LOVED…………….17
LOVE BE WITH YOU…...8	BOREDOM………….…...18
FROM ME TO YOU……..9	TODAY………………..…18
LOVE IS………………..10	MY LIFE…..……………...19
I HOPE……………......10	LIFE IS WHAT YOU MAKE IT ……………….20
I'LL WAIT IN HOPE…….11	LIFE …………………...20
I MISS YOU ………….....12	THINGS …………..…….21
IN LOVE WITH YOU ….13	FUTURE….……..……....21
CRUSH………………..13	

TABLE OF CONTENTS
CONTINUED

DANCE 21

NIGHTIES 22

A LITTLE TWIT 22

PLAY............................23

YOUNG MEN................23

CLASS OF '84 23

IT'S BEEN REAL............24

THANKS MRS. ANDEBRHAN...............25

BEING AT WORK 25

A HOPE.......................26

HARD TIMES................26

FEELINGS....................27

A SMILE......................28

HIDDEN FRIENDSHIP......28

NO REASON...............29

YOUR FRIEND AND I.......29

FRIENDSHIP 29

LOVE ME & LEAVE ME...30

WRONG.....................30

TIRED OF TRYING..........31

I THINK OF YOU............31

BEING ALONE..............32

MISSING YOU..............33

I WANT US TO BE MARRIED...................33

AFTER MARRIAGE.........34

MARRIAGE..................35

I THOUGHT...BUT, I DON'T KNOW............36

MISCELLANEOUS RHYMES....................37

WATCHING YOU

In case you haven't noticed
I like you a lot
I can't say it's love
When it's really not

But, I can say I like you
And that you are my heart
And if I ever get you
We will never be apart

I'll always think of you
As my one and only joy
Until you're a man
'Cause you're only a boy

But, don't let the word "boy"
Tear you apart
Because you'll always have a place
Inside my lonely heart

I think of you when the skies are cloudy
And even when they're blue
I'll never let a boy nor man
Take the place of you

You're always on my mind
I may be on yours, too
You're something very special
And I'm really beginning to love you!

Your Heart

I want your heart for my own,
For it stays within my mind
It sticks to my Inner-most feelings
Your heart is one of a kind
So, give your heart to me
And let me treasure the key
I'll lock it in an ever-locked door
And I'll love you forever more

Virginity

Be a virgin as long as you can
Don't just lay with any man
Don't let your body go to waste
Wait for the right time and the right place
Take my advise there is no rush
You can wait a while for all that mush
But don't get me wrong, love can make you sing
When done right, it can be a beautiful thing!
So, save yourself in that virgin way
And the right man will come along one day

LOVE CONTRACT

Now that I'm yours and you are mine
breaking up would be a waste of time

in fact if you should mention it
I wouldn't dream of calling it "quits"

However if, of you, I ever get tired
You'll get two week's notice before you get fired

And I ask that the same thing you'll agree
If you ever think of firing me

This contract isn't really necessary
'Cause we'll stay together and even marry

As soon as we're married and sharing a heart
We'll be together until death do we part

My Everything

Of all the guys I've ever met
Loving you is something I'll never forget

You do things to try to get me sore
But, one day you'll respect me more

You won't be mine, I won't be yours
We'll be each other's and that's for sure

You have mixed feelings now and I understand
You also have me in the palm of your hand

To you, now, this may not mean much
But, one day you'll long for my touch

Right now you may not know what's best
But, you'll pick me out from all the rest

And you'll find that you love me, too
'Cause My Everything is just for you

JUST BECAUSE

Just because you are so special
Just because you are so sweet
Just because you are a good person
Just because you are so neat

Just because you are so caring
Just because you are so kind
Just because your ways are pleasing
I want you to be mine

Just because are so sincere
So loving and so kind, too
I honor and respect your ways
And I want to be with you

Just because you are so darling
I've longed for you many days
Just because I love you
And I always will…always

OUR LOVE

Our love is going separate ways
Like two hands on a clock
Our love is like two left feet
One without a sock

I cry myself to sleep some nights
Waiting for your call
I try to get in touch with you
You're out having a ball

I try to talk it over
With my family and friends
They say I shouldn't speak to you
Ever, ever again

But, my heart lies unsober
And I'll love you anyway
But, since apart we are
Apart we will stay

SOONER OR LATER

It's off and on, but, it still exists
My love for you is like a gentle kiss

My hope is built on nothing less
Than being with you, 'cause you're the best

My mind is made up of your name
Without my mind, I'll go in sane

I think at night, but, some day it will be
Together forever…just you and me

So, be yourself for right now
But, I'll get your mind, someway, somehow

You're on your own at the time
But, sooner or later, you will be mine

LOVE BE WITH YOU

I'm either crazy or madly in love
I can't stop thinking about you
Whenever I try it makes me cry
And my whole day turns blue

I don't like feeling anxious for you
But, I don't know what else to do
I'm writing with hopes you will see
That the only one for you is me

I know you love me, too
It's written all over your face
Somewhere is empty in your heart
So, put me in that place

I never thought I'd have to ask
A guy to be with me
But, I guess you are worth it
So, I'm yours without a fee

Bring out the man within the child
Forget about being scared for a while
'Cause life is full of let downs and hurt
But, fear is like dog mess in dirt

So, think about this and do think twice
'Cause chances are a part of life
But, whatever you decide to do
Love will be forever with you

From Me To You

This is coming from me to you
Because my love is really true

Love, happiness, truth and grace
When put together, I see your face

In that face, I see the eyes
That took my heart without surprise

In that surprise, I know you're there
With all your tender love and care

You're gentle and I know it's true
I felt it when I first kissed you

I want you to belong to me
Like water belongs to the deep blue sea

I hope you feel the same way, too
This is coming from me to you!

LOVE IS...

There is a thing a few may miss
A smile, a touch, a favor, a kiss

Love is these things and so much more
Love is a thing that many hope for

Love is a feeling deep down inside
That one in love just cannot hide

Love is sincere and very true
And love is...what I feel for you

I HOPE

I hope our love last longer
Remaining as time goes by
I hope our love grows stronger
And the feelings never die

I hope that things get better
So we can bind and never part
I hope you take this letter
And keep it in your heart

And remember this, for all the more...
A hope is something to live for

I'll Wait In Hope

You'll forget about me when you leave
But just don't forget about the baby
That you put here before you went
And left my life all torn and bent

The child is mine, yours as well
So, while you're traveling take a stop by hell
And see all the fathers who left their child
And found that it wasn't worth the while

So, think about this before you go
Before you say good-bye, say hello
To a broken heart that was broken by you
And to your child that you never knew

If you don't know now you'll never know
That running away is not the way to go
You'll find other girls different from me
You might even make another baby

But, hopefully it won't be that way
I hope you'll write me everyday
I also hope that one day you'll be
With me and the child as a family

I also hope your feelings are true
'Cause I am really going to miss you

I Miss You

Not a day goes by that I don't miss you
I know with all my heart that the feelings are true
You've gone away and left me here
And every day I shed many tears
Because I care for you ever so much
And I miss your soft, warm, loving touch
I know I've never told you this
But, you turn me on with your tender kiss
I love it when your lips touch mine
'Cause you make me feel so devine
Not only do I miss your lips
But, I miss your hands caressing my hips
I felt so close to you at first
But, now my heart's about to burst
I think I'm in love though I may not be
Though it seems that you've forgotten me
So many days I sit and cry
"Why haven't he called?" I wonder why
I know I'm just not in your heart
And I wish we weren't so far apart
That way I can talk to you
To see what you are going to do
'Cause you left me with child
which was very uncool
But, I refuse to be a mother and a father too

In Love With You

You may not believe this though it is true
I've fallen very deeply in love with you
You're a very special person who's taken my heart
I can't stand the thought of us being apart
I don't expect for you to feel the same way
But, I hope your feelings will change some day

Crush

I realize you don't have a clue
That I have a serious crush on you
I know you're older, but, you're very sweet
You're really handsome and dress real neat

You carry yourself in a business way
And I admire you more every day
I know your companion is truly in love
'Cause you're the type of man many dream of

Unless I tell you this I'll never be content
This is not a come-on, but, rather a compliment

A Kiss From You

It's really hard to cope
Without your lips touching mine
So, unless you find it hard to do
Please kiss me one more time

Without your tender kiss
My heart refuses to sing
Without your tender kiss
I haven't anything

I want you in my life
But, there's nothing I can do
I know what I want
So, now it's up to you

A Kiss From Me

Your lips are like an old dead tree
Until you've had a kiss from me
My kiss is like a cotton ball
One peck and you are sure to fall
You're likely to fall on your knees
And then you'll crawl back begging please
You'll beg me to become your wife
'Cause a kiss from me will change your life!

A CHILD AND YOU

I always wanted a child
A little baby girl
I know there is nothing like it
In the whole wide world
If my dream came true
I'd give my thanks to you
I'd give my child love and care
And for you I'd always be there

KIM AND MICHAEL

Kim and Michael were lovers
And so everyone knew
One day Kim had to leave
That really turned Michael blue

But, Michael did not give up
He loved Kim until the end
And with their love together so strong
They were back together again

If Tomorrow Comes Too Late

If tomorrow comes too late
And you've left me for good
I'll never get to say the things
That I never could

My feelings hide within
I never tell what I feel
I see a bag full of love
But, you'll never know it's real

Until I tell you of my love
You'll never know it's there
I keep my feelings to myself
You'll never know that I care

So, I've decided to tell you how I feel
On a very special date
I'm going to tell you of my love
In case tomorrow comes too late

If Tomorrow Never Comes

If tomorrow never comes
I'll live for today
I'll have nothing to hope for
Nothing much to say
One day, I'll be a child
The same day, I'll be a mother
I'll live for *today*,
Because there will never be another

I Am Loved

Some days when I don't feel so fine,
I'm with someone I know is mine.
He's right beside me day and night;
He holds my hand with all His might.
He picks me up when I am down;
I am so glad that He's around.
He makes me feel like someone new
Whenever I am sad and blue.
He knows my troubles before they come;
He gives me knowledge to be someone.
He satisfies my every need;
This really is a friend indeed.
He is a spirit from above;
And He lets me know that *I Am Loved*.

BOREDOM

When I am bored
With nothing to do
And where there's fun
I haven't a clue

When I'm off work
And there's no school
And I'm like water
Without a pool

I think of you
In any way
No matter how
It makes my day

TODAY

Today is just
a day that is gone
Tomorrow will come
but I'll just live on
But, *Today* is sharp
As sharp as a knife
'Cause it's the first day
of the rest of my

Love, Life, and Relationships — Grace LaJoy Henderson

My Life

It all started when I was a child
My family did things that were wild
My dad cheated and beat my mother
But, mom kept loving us like no other
I had many problems inside of me
But, no one knew, no one could see
After high school to my surprise
I got a girl pregnant, I could've died!
I was afraid to have a baby, but she kept it anyhow
So, I joined the Navy and look at me now
I married her and left her, which hurt a lot
I thought marriage was the answer; it was not
I started drinking just the same
I thought that it could ease my pain
So, I turned to the streets and sold a few drugs
I hung out with all kinds of thugs
My life became a living hell
And then…I ended up in jail

LIFE IS WHAT YOU MAKE IT

Life is what you make it
You get out of life what you put in
So, if it seems you never win
Take a look at your life
Search deep within

Yes, life is what you make it
So, sow some good seeds
Say some nice words
Do some good deeds

Try these things
When you get up the nerves
'Cause a person only gets
What a person deserves

LIFE

Take advantage of life, It's all around you
You may try to run from problems
You'll never escape
Problems exist in life
As long as life exists, problems will follow
In your mind – feelings hide
Feelings – A part of life
The attitude you take
Reflects upon people in life
Everything – is life itself

THINGS

Looking *back* into time
Those things aren't worth a dime
The things that are *now* will do you good somehow
But the things that are *then* will never be again

FUTURE

It seems to be that all we have
Is the day ahead; which we long to do
Is hope for it to come; which it may never…
Without hope for tomorrow,
We look behind…and live
After our worries are over, where are the dreams?
Do we not have any?
Have we put our early accomplishments ahead?
Or have we not confidence in ourselves?
We need to strive more clearly
So that regret won't steal us

DANCE

Don't fight the feeling, 'cause it feels so good
Just dance to the beat, like the party people would
Let the floor be yours, give the rhythm your feet
Get all into the music,
like you're eating spiced meat

Nighties

Nighties are clothes a small child wears to bed
They could consist of clothes to wear
on arms, legs, even head
They shouldn't be worn out of the home
They're made for bed and not for roam
They're not to be considered "Sunday's best"
Instead they should be worn
during a good night's rest

A "Little Twit"

To do something silly and just don't quit
Is grounds for being a "Little Twit"
A "Little Twit" does awful things
There is no stop to the headaches they bring
They play a part in most every dispute
However, sometimes, they can be cute
One night a "Little Twit" was drinking a coke
All of a sudden he began to choke
His doctor was called, his mom awoke
It turned out to be just a joke
Nerve-wrecking, but, clever, I must admit
It takes hard work to be a "Little Twit"

Play

With all the excitement of today
I must stay in, no time for play
I have a lot of work to do
Maybe tomorrow I'll play with you

Young Men

I walk through the halls
of Westport High
Checking out young men
as they walk by
I only check them out,
but, they're not for me
However, most are nice,
I will agree

Class of '84

I am a student of Westport High
And I can never tell a lie
Class of '84 is on the one
We're almost finished, but, we've just begun
When we are through you'll miss us, but hey!
Remember us in a special way

Love, Life, and Relationships Grace LaJoy Henderson

It's Been Real

Though it's my first year at Westport High
It's really been real and I'll tell you why

I'll start with my first hour teacher, Mr. Ballentyne
He's straight out with his feelings every time

My second hour teacher, coach Murphy is one
Who's almost finished yet's just begun

Mrs. Neuhaus, It's rather hard to reach her
Though she's a very good third hour teacher

Mrs. Beene has something none other has
A very conductive 4th hour foods class

And again 5th hour there's Mr. Ballentyne
Who is very stern, yet very kind

My 6th hour class compares with none
'Cause Mr. Hicks makes it rather fun

Not to forget Mr. Walker
Who punishes me for being a talker

Last, but not least, there's Mrs. Swift
Who runs this school as if it were a gift

With all my heart I say still
It has been most definitely real

Thanks Mrs. Andebrhan

JMG wouldn't be a thing
Without you, as one who leads.
You made it work for all of us.
And now we'll surely succeed!

We'll miss you when it's over.
We'll be leaving at the end
With hopes we can come back
To see you once again.

We want to say, "Thank You"
But, we don't know where to begin.
Well…Thanks for being an inspiration.
And Thanks…For being a friend!

Being at Work

Being at work can get real rough
So we much be patient, but, yet be tough
When I say "tough", I don't mean rude
I mean we should try to keep a good mood
We should be cheerful no matter what
Because there's nothing that we can't cut
The day might attempt to get us down
But, we must never wear a frown
If we look at things positively
We'll find that whatever will be, will be
If we take seriously the words in this letter
Our bad days at work will be a lot better

A Hope

A hope is a desire that comes from the mind
When a person wants something of any kind
Never hope for something you'll never get
Or belongs to someone else, or that you'll regret

A hope is also made to give
Someone something for which to live
After future plans have suited you
A hope will help you carry them through
But, to hope for something that is bad for you
Is to shatter the good it was made to do

Hard Times

When times are hard
And things are rough
Keep your cool
And act real tough
Instead of bringing yourself down
Take things one step at a time
With each step things will brighten up
And you won't lose your mind

FEELINGS

Your feelings mean a lot
To someone who loves you
Your feelings tie a knot
Around your enemies too

You—are your feelings
Nothing can compare
You—are good people
As long as you care

When you begin to hate
Your feelings go to waste
People will not wait
They leave and close the gate

You'll feel lost inside
Your feelings will not hide
You'll look the way you feel
Especially when you cry

A Smile

If you can't find a word to say
A smile can make a person's day.

A smile is gentle and very strong,
And it can last a whole day long.

Smiling can make a frown turn blue;
Why that is, I haven't a clue.

A smile is also very contagious;
That's what makes them so outrageous.

So if you haven't smiled today,
Take my advice and don't delay!

Hidden Friendship

You never know who is your friend
Until the moment at the end

They'll say they'll miss you- then good-bye
And then they'll go somewhere and cry

That person loved you for so long
But, you never knew and now you're gone

No Reason

I am surprised you actually
Dislike a loving person like me
I'm very nice and very sweet
The kind of person you'll love to meet
My friendship comes with no real cost
If you refuse it, it's your lost
However, you chose the wrong way to go
Disliking someone you don't even know

Your Friend and I

I know you probably think
That I'm messing with your friend
But, if that's what you think
It's best you think again

He and I are friends
No more and no less
I would never mess with him
Because I like you best

Friendship

It's always easy to put your all
into a special friendship
The hard part is saying "good-bye"
to that special friend

LOVE ME & LEAVE ME

You let me down, and you're not around
To see the frown, that I've befound
One day you came, and took my fame
With your serious game, and showed no shame
I seek the day, to find a way
To get over all the games you play
Just like a kid, your sincere was hid
I'll never forget the things that you did
I've never met anyone like you
The thoughts remain, the memories, too
You lied in my face with disgust and disgrace
I long for you to be put in your place
And all that time, I thought you were mine
You were really kind, but, you dogged me blind

WRONG

As the days grow cold, as skies are blue
I haven't yet stopped thinking of you
I think of you morning, day, noon, and night
And miss you 'til the next day's light
To hold you again is how I've longed
But, all you do is do me wrong

Tired of Trying

My mommy always told me
When I tried and didn't win
"If at first you don't succeed,
try, try again"

So, I'm trying this last time
To win your stubborn heart
And if this time I don't succeed
We'll just have to be apart

Yes, I'm trying one more time
The choice is up to you
'Cause I refuse to be a fool
And keep running after you

I Think of You

As the night grows cold
I think of you
And wonder what
I'm going to do
To get you back
Into my arms
So you can fill me
With your charm

BEING ALONE

It's not very fun to be alone
No one to talk to on the phone

You're trapped in a door
With the key thrown away
Hoping not to be alone some day

But, if love never comes
And you still exist
You'll think of the love
That you have missed

So straighten your life
'Cause it's just begun
And you won't end up
With no one

Missing You

Daydreaming of the nights
That softly I would kiss you
Crying all the time
Because I really miss you
Waking up in a passionate cry
After sensual dreams of you and I

That's an example of how my life's been
While awaiting the day that you'll hold me again
Never thinking that I could miss a man so much
I sit here in starvation, I'm hungry for your touch
Crazy I know it seems, but, all is true
And it's all in the life of Missing You

I Want Us To Be Married

Without the warmth of you
I feel so all alone
I want us to be married
So you can be my own

I don't want cheap sex
Because that is a sin
I want us to be married
Otherwise, we'll never win

After Marriage

I see a vision of us, we're very much in love
We've just gotten married,
It's a blessing from above
It is a very bright and sunny afternoon
and we're getting ready to go on our honeymoon

Oh! There we are again, we're on our honeymoon
We're waiting for our wine
It will be here very soon
We're in a nice hotel and having lots of fun
The baby is asleep and the night has just begun

Well, our honeymoon is over,
We're in our nice, new home
It's in a quiet neighborhood
In a little town near Rome

Happily married are we, we kiss, we hug, we talk
We even hold hands when we're on our daily walk

The children are very happy
They're enrolled in private schools
They're very well disciplined
'Cause *you* make all the rules

We just had our fifth little baby
He's in a brass baby carriage
Well, there you have my fantasy
of us…After Marriage

MARRIAGE

Marriage is a gift....
And can only work when God plays a part
Of the persons lives and is in their heart.

Problems are needed to make a marriage stronger.
Overcoming problems makes a marriage last longer.

A marriage should be loving and caring.
A marriage is made of giving and sharing.

Working together and "hangin' in"
Is easy if the two are clever.
With understanding and no demanding,
A marriage can last forever.

The first goal....Put your mates needs first
In everything you do
The second goal....Is to be Happy
Faithful, Honest and True

A marriage is strengthened through laughs and cries;
With work there will never be any good-byes.
But, if ever one's discouraged, and thinks of someone new,
Just think of the second goal,
to be Faithful, Honest and True.

My closing are words to keep in your heart;
A marriage won't stand without God as a part.

So, make your marriage the best it can be;
And may blessings be with your family!!

I Thought… But, I Don't Know

I'm writing this letter as a child
Who knows ZIP about love
Who knows nothing about caring
A child who's just in "WUV"
I thought I knew so much
But, I realize my mind is so brittle
I thought I was ready for love
But, I realize I know so little
You deserve someone to love you
The way you ought to be
A person who can care for you
A person unlike me
The love is there
But, I don't know how to use it
The right word is there
But, I don't know how to choose it
I thought it would be easy
"Living the Married Life"
But, I don't know how to have a husband
Let alone…be a wife
It's not that I don't love you
I just don't know how to treat you
It's not that I don't want you
I just don't know how to keep you
So, until we are older
And have had more preparation
The best thing for us
Is a legal separation

Miscellaneous Rhymes

I look at him, then look at you
I try my best to compare the two
But, I find it hard to really compare
When one plays games and one really cares

~~~~~~

Though my feelings remain the same
My heart lies in tears
Because my love for you
Has turned into fears

~~~~~~

I hope you put some thought into this
And don't just throw it away
Because we may have tomorrow
Since we messed up yesterday

Love, Life, and Relationships   Grace LaJoy Henderson

Books and Resources by Grace LaJoy

A Gifted Child in Foster Care: *A Story of Resilience*
(Book, Teacher's Guide, Student Workbook)

Writer's Breakthrough:
Steps To Copyright and Publish Your Own Book (Book)

More Than Mere Words: *Poetry That Ministers*
(Christian Poetry Book)

Unmerited Favor: 101 Quotes of Wisdom, Inspiration, and God's Grace

Social Inspirations: *Christian Quotes for Life* By Aric J. Henderson

Poetic Empowerment (Spoken Word CD)

Poetic Book Series: Diversity in our Schools, Diversity in our Workplace, The Bad Butt Kids, He's Worth It

Sexual Purity and the Young Woman:
A Guide to Sexual Purity (Book)

Understanding Each Other:
A Guide for Parents and their Children (Book)

My Automobile Dealership (Book)

Diversity and My Credit Union (Book)

An Urgent Call to the Power of Ministry:
Realizing your ministry through your life experiences (Book)

Tapping Into the Gifts, Talents, and Learning Styles of Special Education Students by Arlivia S. White and Grace LaJoy Henderson (Book)

A New Kind of Hustle by Dr. Sugar Lee Lewis with Dr. Grace LaJoy

To learn more please visit us online at
www.gracelajoy.com

www.ingramcontent.com/pod-product-compliance
Lightning Source LLC
Chambersburg PA
CBHW071846290426
44109CB00017B/1944